Tur... Vision

power * passion * purpose

<small>COACH</small> JOSH NIBLETT

<small>With</small> G. Tom Ward

Copyright 2014
G. Tom Ward

All rights reserved. This book is the original work by the author,
and may not be reproduced in any way
or manner without the express
written consent of either author G. Tom Ward or 4Ward Books

ISBN-13: 978-1500948306

ISBN-10: 1500948306

Part of the Winners 2.0 Series
By 4Ward Books

TABLE OF CONTENTS

THIS BOOK IS DEDICATED

To the God whom I serve

and

To the family I love

Tunnel Vision

Prologue

The Halftime

E verything that a team could possibly lose in one game was on the line.

Coach Josh Niblett sprinted, with his team, off the field of the Hoover Met, through the tunnel, and into the locker room.

The first half of the state playoff semi-finals had been an unmitigated disaster. Hoover trailed 21-10. His Bucs had allowed a blocked punt for the first time in his six years at the helm of the team. They had been outplayed on offense, defense, and special teams.

As the players filed into the locker room, they understood that every goal for their year could evaporate into the chilly November air.

Hoover Bucs Head Football Coach Josh Niblett leads his team during the 2013 national championship season.

Unless they could overcome a 21-10 halftime deficit, the Hoover Bucs would lose...

    **A second consecutive state championship;

    **A second consecutive undefeated season;

    **A chance at the national championship... never before won

by Hoover;

   **A four-year undefeated streak at their Hoover Met. No player in the program had ever lost a home game.

To make things even worse, the team handing them a first-half beating was none other than their arch-rival, the Vestavia Hills High School Rebels.

Playing from behind at home was not exactly routine, so their coach understood the importance of leadership at this moment.

Fans cheer as Niblett's Hoover Bucs storm out of the tunnel and onto the field at the Hoover Met.

"A large part of leadership is convincing people to believe in themselves," Niblett explained. "I knew they had the ability to come back. Our entire coaching staff knew they could do it. The key was helping our players put everything in perspective.

"They just had to focus on the moment...on their role in the very next play," Niblett added. "They needed tunnel vision, focusing on each play rather than worrying about the scoreboard or the fans."

In other words, they needed leadership.

Niblett stood to speak. He glanced around at his players, quickly discerning the mood of their locker room.

Niblett saw players waiting eagerly for his words. Everyone knew what was at stake. Everyone knew that no player on the team had ever lost a home game. Everyone knew that they couldn't merely outplay Vestavia now; they had to beat an excellent team by at least two scores in the second half.

Everyone knew that they had to band together to become greater than the sum of their parts.

5

"We don't have to go out like this," he began, as the team listened intently.

"This isn't just any team; this is Hoover," Niblett continued. "We play football by a standard. We spend the off season reaching for that standard, and we practice by that standard every day. When game time comes, we're ready to play to that standard."

He paused, and looked around the room at the players and coaches. "But it's more than just football. We live our lives by that standard. That's what makes our team unique.

"If you don't want to go out like this...if you don't want the season to end tonight...the answer is simple. All you have to do is go out there and play every single moment of this game to the standard that we have set together.

"That's it. If you do that, we'll be alright."

According to Niblett, the focus on each play rather than the scoreboard, the tunnel vision required by each player, fits in perfectly with their team's philosophy and his beliefs as a coach.

Josh Niblett and his son Shaw pose with the national championship trophy, which would not have been won without the historic comeback win over Hoover's arch rival Vestavia.

"We just want our destiny as a team to depend on what we do... not what our opponents do, or what someone on the outside does," Niblett explained.

So how hard would it be to stage a comeback against the Vestavia Rebels?

"They're the worst type of team to play from behind," Niblett said while shaking his head. "They have a powerful running attack, so it's easier for them to run down the clock and give us less time for a comeback. Buddy Anderson is a great coach, and he doesn't care whether it's 4th-and-1, or 3rd-and-15; he'll run the ball if he wants to. They have a stable of excellent running backs, and Buddy uses them perfectly."

So did the rousing remarks by Niblett work perfectly?

"Hardly," he said with a laugh. "Vestavia came out and scored to open the third quarter. Then we trailed 28-10. Things were not looking up for us."

Despite the coach's self deprecating humor, Niblett's Bucs did precisely what he asked them to do in the second half.

After the opening drive, the Hoover defense stifled the Vestavia attack and allowed their own team more opportunities to score.

Niblett (center) teaches drills for Hoover fullbacks running pass routes out of the backfield during 2014 spring practice. According to Niblett, the commitment to focus on every aspect of the game is a critical element of success.

And that's exactly what they did. Three touchdowns later, the 28-10 deficit was transformed into a historic 31-28 comeback victory.

Hoover vs. Vestavia has long been one of the greatest American rivalries, but on a November night in 2013, the tunnel vision of Bucs players empowered their team to perhaps the greatest comeback in school history.

When discussing the comeback over their arch rival, Niblett speaks less of the game itself and more about the word "why."

"In my heart, I believe that no one outworks us," he said more factually than speculatively. "I really believe our work ethic is second to none, but it's not just about working hard.

"It's one thing to be told what to do, and better to be told how to do it. But if you understand 'why' you're doing it, you're actually learning.

"We work hard to teach our players why they're doing what they're doing. When adversity comes, and you're down by 18 points to a great team in the second half, you'll understand why you worked so hard leading up to that game. You'll understand the skills you have, and you'll understand that you'll have the ability to make good things happen in the game.

"You'll also understand that the game depends on what you and your team do, rather than what anyone on the outside does.

"It all comes down to focusing on what is most important."

Simply put, it's all about TUNNEL VISION.

It all began with a newspaper

Running through the tunnel to mount great comebacks and win games originated long before the years at Hoover High School.

Actually, it all began with a newspaper.

The Niblett boys, Tad and Josh, prepared to run through the tunnel leading from the locker room to the football field. As they readied themselves for the game, they knew they would sprint from the tunnel onto the field as they burst through the large banner held by cheerleaders.

Tonight was game night, and the two sons of Head Coach John Niblett wanted nothing more than to lead their dad's team to victory.

It was a scene they had played in their minds many times, and they would not let their dad down tonight.

Indeed, they would not play at all that night because Tad was five years old and brother Josh was three. That wouldn't stop them from pretending, and it wouldn't stop them from running through the tunnel and crashing through the banner. Their one-year-old sister, Heather, had already begun her role as cheerleader in her brothers' games...a role that would continue all the way through high school.

On this day, and every day back then, the tunnel was the den in the Niblett home, and the banner was a newspaper held by their sweet mom, Brenda.

"I would hold the newspaper," Brenda recalled, "and they would run through it with all the energy and zeal of the players on Friday night."

In those days, tunnel vision meant the joy of practicing for the future joy of running onto the field with their dad. As they grew, and as they began running through that tunnel each autumn Friday night, their goals, their lives, and the meaning of tunnel vision changed.

TUNNEL VISION, literally, as the Hoover Bucs emerge from the tunnel of the Hoover Met to adoring fans.

For Josh Niblett, the tunnel vision continued long past high school. The childhood dream of running through the stadium tunnel, onto the football field, became a new quest during college.

Niblett's dad, Coach John Niblett, understood his son's dreams. "When Josh transferred from Southern Miss, he was highly recruited by several schools. However, he wanted to run through that tunnel for the University of Alabama."

And that, John Niblett explained, led to other dreams. "Once Josh achieved his dream of running through that tunnel for the Crimson Tide, it was no longer enough. He had achieved his dream, so now he wanted more. Next, he was determined to play and contribute to the team. Nothing was going to stand in his way."

For Josh Niblett, the idea of tunnel vision is much more than a catchy theme for a book. The importance of focus on God, family, football, friends, and success, has defined his life.

"Becoming focused, and staying focused, is the key to excellence," Niblett added. "In order to do that, you have to be able to answer three basic questions about everything you do to become better."

9

1. WHAT?

Josh Niblett and his older brother Tad already knew what to do; they just imitated their dad, the football coach.

They were too young to understand it, but Tad and Josh Niblett began preparing for success long before starting kindergarten.

Because they knew what they wanted to do, they began envisioning that goal as reality. They began preparing for the goal as something that stood in their future.

For Niblett's Hoover Bucs, the "what" involves learning the playbook. The "what" involves a life of exercise and diet and strengthens the body and spirit. The "what" involves studying schoolwork with the same zeal that one studies the playbook. The "what" involves learning that it's not the will to win, but rather the will to prepare to win that matters.

An important part of succeeding is understanding what success really means. That means answering the question of "what" you're looking to become. In the pages of *Tunnel Vision*, you'll see a road map for success in every area of your life. You have the potential, today, for growth and success in your pursuits, your career, your relationships, your impact on others, your self-improvement, and your spiritual core (which is who you really are).

Tunnel Vision is about much more than setting goals; the priorities of your life are more about who you are and whom you aspire to become.

2. HOW?

Understanding "what" Josh Niblett wanted to do is the easy part. Most readers could probably guess many of his goals without reading the pages of *Tunnel Vision*.

Josh Niblett wanted to succeed in athletics, make good grades in school, play on championship teams, play college ball, marry the girl of his dreams, raise great kids, succeed as a coach, and most of all live a life that reflects his love and commitment to Jesus Christ in all things.

Pretty basic stuff, right?

If it's nothing unusual, then why do so few people achieve those goals? Why has Josh Niblett succeeded so grandly?

What separates Niblett from so many others who have spent their lives aspiring to the same goals?

For Niblett and his Hoover Bucs, the "how" involves looking at every practice as an opportunity to become better rather than a chore. The "how" involves treating school homework as a chance to become better educated and successful rather than some boring assignment. The "how" involves treating every meal as a chance to improve and fuel your body rather than an opportunity to indulge it with junk.

The answer to "how" is to remain focused on the process by which the "what" can become reality.

The answer is Tunnel Vision.

3. WHY?

"So many people know what to do, and they figure out how to do it, but then they quit," Niblett added. "The 'why' is the question that so many people miss, and it's really the key to success."

The Hoover High School gym is silent, except for two men having a quiet conversation. John Niblett, the dad of Hoover coaches Josh and Tad, is giving an interview to the co-author of this book. The interview began at a different volume, because it involved two men with vibrant voices...the types of voices that got them in trouble as children because the teachers always heard them above the others in class.

So why were they speaking quietly during the interview?

As they spoke, roughly a hundred football players filed into the gym and sat in the bleachers with the men while waiting on their coaches.

Their spring football game would begin within the next hour or so. The co-author focused on the subject of the interview, but did not miss the fact that a hundred football players had entered the gym with no supervising coaches but remained almost silent while waiting for their leaders.

Looking around, one could see quiet whispers between players, but nothing could be heard. The kids appeared happy and enthused about the game. They were just disciplined to behave as a team.

Underneath a giant poster of the senior football Bucs, Hoover Bucs fans wait in line for admission into the opening game of the national championship 2013 season.

The Hoover Bucs celebrate their 2009 epic comeback win over Camden County High School in Georgia. The fourth quarter was carried live by ESPN, which interrupted its regularly scheduled programming.

This was a spring game, a glorified practice. This was not the state championship game. It wasn't even a regular season affair.

Yet there they were. Not silent, but extremely quiet.

Any coach could make kids be silent, but it's much more difficult to let them talk but maintain serenity while mentally preparing for a game.

In that one moment, the aura of Hoover football could be clearly understood. The confidence of national and state championships, joined by a rare level of discipline, converged into a rushing stream of success.

The scene in the gym, and the success of Hoover football, raised many questions. Each one seemed to begin with the word "why."

WHY were these high school kids so much more disciplined than most...and WHY were they able to seem so happy in doing so?

WHY is it that some organizations, whether in sports or in business, can enjoy success while others just can't seem to make it happen?

WHY is it that Josh Niblett seems so completely unaffected by his success?

WHY do the students seem so hungry to win, even after all of the championships?

For Niblett, the most important part of it all is the willingness to ask and seek the answer to the question: "WHY?"

"The quitters want to know WHAT, the campers want to know HOW, and the climbers want to know WHY," Niblett began. "If we don't understand the answer to that question, we'll never become all that we can be.

Becoming all we can be gave rise to the concept of *Tunnel Vision*. As co-author G. Tom Ward described the book to Dr. Jane Geiger, they discussed the title. The desire to run through the tunnel, into the arena, had been Josh Niblett's goal since infanthood. Several times, when telling the Niblett story, the word "tunnel" was used. Then, she pitched a simple yet profound idea.

"How about *Tunnel Vision* as the title?"

Ward put down his salad fork and picked up the title of the book. Niblett was immediately on board, and the project accelerated.

Dr. Buddy Gray, also interviewed for Tunnel Vision, heartily approved of the title and the concept.

For Niblett, the idea of *Tunnel Vision* brought together the answers to WHAT, WHY, and HOW with each of the coaching jobs in which he has served.

"At Oneonta High School, my first coaching job, we had great success. I loved the school, the people, and especially my players. It was great and we won big, but I still didn't understand the answer to the question of WHY I was doing what I was doing. I was still stuck in HOW to do things.

"In Oxford, we were blessed with success and we loved it there too, but I was still stuck in wanting to know what to do and how to do it."

At Hoover, given the size of the school and the magnificent history, Niblett faced a different set of challenges.

"I was forced to search for the answer to the question of WHY. Most of these players, and certainly the administrators and fans, had already tasted success. They already knew one way to win and how to get there. The first thing we wanted to inject into the program was a vision of WHY we want to succeed."

The WHY has produced six consecutive trips to the state championship game.

The WHY has produced three state championships. This past year, the WHY has produced Hoover's first national championship.

As you learn to ask WHAT, HOW, and WHY, you'll begin developing the type of focus that will help you succeed.

You will develop *Tunnel Vision*.

Tunnel Vision

Chapter 1

Focus on Excellence

Iron sharpens iron

You may have heard the expression before. You may have even used it before.

If you want to completely understand it, look no further than the Hoover Bucs football team.

It's so easy to see on the Hoover sidelines. The coaches implement the game plan yet adapt collaboratively via headphones to each play in the game.

All the coaches participate. All the coaches contribute. After all, national championships are not won without a staff filled with excellent coaches.

However, two of the coaches speak a little differently to each other.

The first quarter was halfway over. The Hoover Bucs have the ball, but they hadn't had much luck so far. Although the defense had played well, the offense had gotten off to a slow start, and the coaches were ready to score.

"Tad, let's run play action to set up that bubble screen," Josh Niblett said into his headphones, though with his voice, the headphones are hardly necessary for those on the sidelines.

Josh Niblett doesn't stand still on the sidelines any more than he does anywhere else. Tad paced just as much, though his voice is more difficult to hear for those not on the headphones.

Unlike most other seasons, the Hoover Bucs of 2014 run to set up the pass, rather than passing to set up the run. The new paradigm, successful because of the personnel, sometimes requires more patience from the coaches. That's especially true early in the game.

One reason for the run-based offense is the stable of tailbacks, led by one who will soon be carrying the ball for one of the many colleges who have offered him a scholarship. He's not the only talented back, and the college recruiters know it.

Finally, the Hoover Bucs scored and grabbed the lead. They would never relinquish that lead, as it would grow to a 35-7 score by halftime.

The crowd went wild.

The intense coaches were momentarily relieved.

The cheerleaders led chants and did flips.

College scouts sat in the bleachers and leaned against the fence near the field.

The game had everything one could ask from a crisp, Friday night of an Alabama autumn.

Only it was neither a Friday, a night, nor autumn.

The crowd, the college scouts, and the intensity were all part of the Hoover spring game against a visiting team from South Alabama.

Iron sharpens iron.

It's the foundation of the daily effort of excellence within the Hoover football program.

Iron sharpens iron.

The Niblett boys became aspiring coaches at young ages.

It sounds like a simple statement, but the expression has been extant in Josh Niblett's life since he was a baby.

While he was still in diapers, Josh Niblett's life of excellence began by iron sharpening iron...thanks to his big brother, Tad.

If you planned to sharpen a knife or a sword, would you use something dull or soft as a sharpener? Of course not. You would use a hard metal device to make your knife or sword as sharp as possible.

In many ways, we are much like swords or knives. We need to be sharpened by something that is of high quality; we remain dull if we depend on people or things that are soft or dull.

For Niblett, it began as soon as he was able to play with his older brother, Tad.

The two boys were inseparable. They played baseball in the summers. They played football in the fall and into the winter. They played basketball in the winter and during March Madness. No matter the season, they played hard and they played to beat each other.

"Tad was two years older, but I didn't care. I played to beat him at any game."

For Tad, the competition was just as fierce. "I could usually beat Josh when we were younger, but that didn't stop him from believing he could win."

17

Their little sister, Heather, grew up with a front seat view of the daily competition. "It's hard to imagine two brothers being closer but also so competitive," she said with a laugh. "One minute, they were best friends, the next minute they fought, and a moment later they were best friends again."

Brenda Niblett knows better than anyone how early the football fanaticism began. "The boys always related things to sports," she recalled fondly. "We walked into the First Baptist Church of Opelika when they were little. Josh pointed to the balcony and said he wanted to sit in the upper deck."

Tad (left) and Josh (right) served as ballboys for their dad's teams.

Tad remembers the dreams of running through the tunnel and playing for the game. "We had one of those old tape recorders," Tad explained. "We would hit the 'record' button and make crowd noise. Then, we would play back our crowd noise on the tape player while we played football. Our mom would hold newspapers up, and we would pretend to run through the tunnel and through the banner onto the field. We loved every minute of it."

So when the Niblett boys played football, they had a newspaper banner, recorded crowd noise, and of course their little sister Heather cheering on the sidelines. "They always included me," Heather recalled, "unless I got in the way."

Josh Niblett grew up competing with an older brother in everything. He wanted to throw the ball like Tad did. He wanted to understand football as well as Tad did. He wanted to run faster than Tad did.

When the Niblett boys reached elementary school, they impatiently wanted to practice with their dad's football team each day.

Ever the encourager, their mom would dress the boys in shoulder pads, helmets, and football jerseys each day. Then, she would drop them off at the practice sessions of their dad's team. Tad and Josh would do exercises and calisthenics with the team, and then watch from the sidelines as the team practiced.

Every day, on the field, in the gym, and in the classroom, Tad and Josh competed. They made each other better.

John Niblett remembers one car ride in which Tad challenged Josh in an unusual way. "I heard Tad tell Josh he was going to tell on him, and Josh didn't like it. I asked them what was going on, and Tad said that he heard Josh's bedtime prayers the night before. He said Josh prayed to score touchdowns but didn't pray for the entire team."

He chuckled at the story, but then explained its importance. "That story shows how much they cared about excellence," John explained. "Tad cared that Josh prayed about the right things. Josh learned important lessons about teamwork, and about how actions affect other people. Both of them still remember that well."

John Niblett (center), a retired coach, stands proudly with his two sons Josh (left) and Tad (right). Josh and Tad have prepared for coaching careers since their days as toddlers in the Niblett home.

Recognizing his boys' love for sports, their dad also decided to challenge them while they were still children.

Coach John Niblett not only let his boys exercise with the team, he taught them what it meant to become part of a team.

"Dad wanted to challenge us at an early age," Tad added. "He could see that we were both competitive, so he honored that by raising us to love competition and excellence."

"My boys were learning things at a young age that put them way ahead of other kids in terms of sports," explained John Niblett. "They taught each other how to compete, and I taught them how to play the games."

One of the Niblett children, however, seemed to be slightly outside hearing range of their dad's voice. "When Heather played softball and basketball," Brenda Niblett recalled, "John was like a lot of parents in that he would coach from the stands. Heather always played her game and pretended not to hear him. It really was funny. Tad and Josh said they never could have gotten away with that."

As the boys grew older, the competition continued. Then, however, it often involved their playing on the same teams against other schools.

19

John Niblett smiled when asked about the boys playing on the same team. "When Tad was a senior, Josh was a freshman. Tad played quarterback, Josh played receiver, and Heather was a cheerleader. It was a special time."

After Friday night football games, most high school football players enjoy going out, being with friends, and hopefully celebrating victories as local celebrities.

Not the Niblett boys.

Josh laughed when asked about his Friday nights. "Tad and I did exactly what we wanted to do. We spent Friday nights breaking down game film with dad."

Tad agreed. "That's what we wanted to be doing on Friday nights. We wanted to improve as players. We wanted to challenge each other. We wanted to help our team be better."

"They both had natural ability, but a lot of kids have ability," their dad added. "They succeeded because they made each other better."

Brenda Niblett believes the seriousness with which they approached sports played a large role in their making each other better. "They challenged each other constantly, whether in football, basketball, or baseball.

"When they were young, they were always so serious about whatever they were playing. When they would play Wiffle ball, they would take flour and line off the field like a baseball field. When they played basketball, they would record and interview into a cassette player. One would be the player, and one would be the commentator."

Heather, who was usually the cheerleader, enjoyed the games as much as her brothers. Today, she and her husband Bob live in Alabaster (AL), where they're raising their three boys-- Reese, Carter, and Graham. They've been deeply entrenched in the community, and especially Westwood Baptist Church, for over 15 years...but that doesn't keep them from supporting the Hoover Bucs.

Although their boys will ultimately attend high school at Hoover's rival Thompson, Reese has served as a Hoover ball boy for three years and is completely a part of the team.

"Reese loves being with his uncles Josh and Tad," Heather explained. "His fellow ball boys have been Josh's son Shaw and Tad's son Riley. Now, Riley is old enough to play on Hoovers' team, so that will be even more fun now.

"For the state championship game, which Hoover has played every year Reese has been a ball boy, our family travels a day early and makes it a fun trip for all the Nibletts. Josh and Tad treat Reese as a full part of the team, and we're so grateful.

"Also, our church family at Westwood supports our family, so they're always telling Bob and me that they're praying for Josh & Tad, that they saw something on TV about Hoover, or that they read a nice article in the paper. They love us, so they love our family."

The Nibletts are already teaching the next generation of their family about teamwork, discipline, and a cause greater than themselves.

That's how success is born.

That's iron sharpening iron.

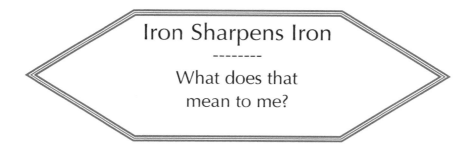

Iron Sharpens Iron

What does that
mean to me?

It's tempting to think that the story of Josh and Tad doesn't mean much to the rest of us. After all, how many brothers are that close in age and talented enough to each win All-State honors in three different sports? How many of us have both the talent, and a talented sibling, to challenge us? How many have two parents so supportive and engaged in challenging and improving? How many aspiring athletes and coaches have a dad and brother who would break down game film on Friday nights together?

Believe it or not, the story of Josh and Tad is not about football. It's not even about sports at all.

Their childhood, their coaching together, their supportive parents, and their careers are a great lesson to us all that is independent of anything athletic.

"It's real simple; iron sharpens iron," Josh explained. "We don't live in this world alone. We have a choice about whom we hang around and the people we associate with. If you want to become better, you have to be around people who challenge you."

Niblett places his fork down on his plate. It's lunch time, and he's clearly enjoying two events at the same time: One of the interviews for this book, and the salad at a *Jason's Deli* in his beloved Hoover.   "I tell my kids that, every day, you're either living or dying." His expression becomes pointed as the passion rises. "It matters who you spend time with. "Too many kids today spend all of their time entertaining themselves instead of growing as people. I read that the average age of video gamers is in the mid-thirties. Video games are great; my kids and our players play them. But if you abuse them, and if you spend your life trying to entertain yourself all the time, your life will be empty."

He leaned forward and clasped his hands. "I love my players. We spend so much time together. I want them to live their lives pursuing excellence. Tad and I had each other, but our players have each other. Every reader of this book will have someone to sharpen them."

So how does someone begin sharpening themselves? How does someone begin pursuing excellence?

Iron Sharpens Iron

Step One
Renew your mind

"We are called to transform ourselves by the renewing of our minds," Niblett said. "The idea of actually transforming ourselves is powerful, but it can happen, and it begins with our minds." (See the 12th chapter of Romans in the Bible)

So how does that happen?

"Begin by reading," he explained. "I don't read as much as I should, but I seek out books by people who have led lives of excellence. I try to find that one nugget of wisdom that will help me improve as a person. I try to find stories or ideas to share with our team. I try to find principles to share with our coaches."

When asked what reading he recommended, Niblett did not hesitate. "The Bible," he replied. "That's the best way to renew your mind. Because I'm in coaching, I enjoy books by successful coaches. Nick Saban has written an excellent book. I really enjoyed Urban Meyer's book. I've read both of Pete Carroll's books and recommend them highly.

"I also read books such as 'Good To Great,' about success in the business world. The fact is that we can never receive too much wisdom."

At the end of this book, you will find a special section that will help you, the reader, renew your mind through the power of God. Favorite readings of Josh Niblett and others are listed and previewed to help you transform yourself in your life.

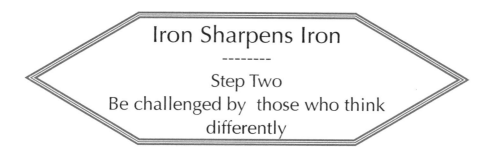

Iron Sharpens Iron

Step Two
Be challenged by those who think differently

As anyone in the Niblett family will tell you, one reason Tad and Josh challenged each other so effectively is because they were so different from each other.

Seriously?

One would imagine they are carbon copies of each other. They are brothers. They are close in age. They spent their childhood together as inseparable teammates at almost everything. Both are sports fanatics. Both were each All-State in three different sports. Both played college football. Both went into coaching, with the ultimate goal of coaching together. They coach together now.

So how different are their personalities?

As different as night and day, according to their mom, "Tad has always been very quiet and calm, but highly competitive."

And Josh?

"Josh was always...well...just Josh," She said after an impish pause. "He is emotional and energetic. They're completely different, and that's why Tad brings out the best in Josh, and Josh brings out the best in Tad."

Tad chuckled when asked to describe the difference between his brother and himself. "Josh wants to be around people 24/7. I would be happy spending hours at a time working on game film or reading. We just charge our batteries in different ways."

Their sister Heather had an A-game when it came to social skills. "When Heather was in the first grade," Brenda explained, "she asked me one day to walk over to the car pickup line after school so she could introduce me to the other moms. When she was young, she shadowed me in the same way that the boys shadowed their dad. We're still really close."

Dealing with people who act and think differently is an important

23

part of sharpening one's mind. People who are interested and interesting can challenge and sharpen.

Also, as Niblett was quick to add, people with different ideas can

The Niblettt boys have been inseparable since childhood...even from the days in the playpen. As anyone on the Hoover Bucs sideline knows, they still communicate in a unique and brotherly way.

prepare you for the critics in life. For the Nibletts, as coaches, it is especially important as they deal with fans, supporters, and the media.

"Hoover has special people and great people, but there will always be people who think differently and criticize," he said with a grin. "We just won the national championship after two years without a loss, but there will always be critics who say we should do this or we shouldn't do that.

"You'll always have some who are jealous, or who think their kids should play more, or that we should do something this way or that way. I don't ask everyone to love us; I just ask that they respect what we're doing."

Iron Sharpens Iron

Step Three
Be a VICTOR,
not a VICTIM

It's your choice.

You face tough times. You face circumstances that are painful or difficult. We all do.

You can be a victim.

You can be an agent of change.

The Niblett family moved, because their dad took a new job. The kids had to start all over in a new school. They had to make new friends. They had to compete on the ball field with kids who were already

24

entrenched in their roles as stars of the team.

The Niblett kids had a choice: They could either become victims, or change agents. According to Dr. Jane N. Geiger, author of *The Obstacle Course*, the "victim or victor" choice is an important lesson for a family to teach children. "Especially for families who move from time to time, teaching them victory over victimhood is a great way to empower children for a healthy and happier future," she added.

The interesting thing is that the Niblett family moved several times, as their dad progressed in his coaching career.

Each time, they thrived.

Each time, they refused to be victims.

Each time, they used the moves to make their family even closer.

"I have always felt guilty that we moved our children so much," explained their mom, Brenda Niblett. "But they agree that it made our family unit stronger. Because when we first moved to different locations, we did not know anyone for a while. We depended on each other more. With three children, there are three personalities. So one might have more trouble adjusting and meeting people than another. But in retrospect I think it made it easier for them in adult life to adjust to changes. No matter where we lived, all three of them always stepped right in and became part of the athletic programs."

So how did the three Niblett kids fare away from playing fields? "They were all salutatorian or valedictorian of their senior class," Brenda added. "They all graduated with honors. So all in all I think it worked out for the best."

Dr. Jane N. Geiger, a family therapist for over 20 years, believes that the success of the Niblett children is a great lesson for us all.

"Moving around yet still enjoying success means that the Nibletts have the ability to adapt and adjust," Geiger explained. "Flexibility is a sign of good mental health, and being rigid in expectations and methods is a sign of poor emotional health. The children of coaches, ministers, and military personnel are known for having to move around. John and Brenda Niblett used the moving to help their family grow closer. They empowered their children for success."

For Josh Niblett, the choice is simple. "Trials and tribulations are a part of life; they're unavoidable," he added. "It's not a matter of whether they will come, but when they will arrive. You can spend each day either living or dying. Our players know each day that they can either improve or step backwards.

"It's your choice."

Tunnel Vision

Chapter 2

Focus on the Future

A defensive back in football can be one of the loneliest positions in all of sports. If you're covering a receiver, you may be the only person who prevents a game-changing play or a game-winning touchdown.

If you cover the receiver well, you can be a hero. However, if you mess up, you could be blamed for losing the game. If you miss a tackle, an average play becomes a big play and a highlight on the local news.

Making plays and avoiding mistakes are critical, but there is one more thing needed by all good defensive backs.

When the big decisions have to be made, the head coach stands alone.

You must learn to put the past behind you.

All players, no matter the skill or position, make mistakes. The problem for defensive backs is that their mistakes are seen by almost everyone. No one has to wonder whether a defensive back has made a big mistake.

The worst thing for any player, and especially for defensive backs, is to line up for the next play while dwelling on the previous play. Mistakes have to be put aside so you can concentrate on the next play. If you can't get over a mistake in the previous play, the next play might bring a bigger one.

In other words, defensive backs must play with tunnel vision, concentrating on the next play and forgetting the past.

Life is so very much like playing defensive back. If you want to live a life of excellence, the worst thing you can do is to concentrate on your previous mistakes.

Learning from Elephants

When the circus comes to town, the workers have to unload large quantities of equipment, tools, stage props, and of course, animals.

Some creatures, like lions or tigers, have to remain caged at all times. As you might imagine, different animals are stored and transported in a variety of different ways.

Amazingly, the largest animals in most circuses, the elephants, are the easiest to transport and contain. If you ever watch a circus unload in a new city, you will notice that most elephants are tied to a post, pole or stake in the ground with a thin rope.

Seriously?

That's right; elephants are contained by small ropes that they could easily rip to shreds.

But how? How do the trainers know they can tie the massive creatures down with a relatively minuscule rope?

The answer lies in Southeast Asia, where elephants have been used for transportation since the dawn of time.

In their infancy, elephants are tied down by large, thick ropes from which the youngsters are unable to break free. They pull, they struggle, they try with all of their underdeveloped might, but the rope poses too large of a challenge.

Ultimately, the elephants give up.

When that happens, the elephants respond to the stimulus of a rope tied around their necks by remaining docile.

There is no more furious pulling.

There is no struggling.

There is no steely determination to break free from the rope that binds.

There is no indefatigable quest for freedom.

In other words, they have given up already, so there is no need to struggle when a rope is tied around their necks.

As a result, adult elephants, in Southeast Asia and in circuses around the world, are tied down by thin ropes.

That suggests a question: Are the elephants tied down by the thin ropes, or are they tied down by their own minds?

Are they tied down by their circumstances, or are they tied down by their belief that they are tied down?

Do you believe that you are tied down by your circumstances?

Could it be your economic circumstances? Is it your family situation?

Is there something in your past, or your present, that you believe ties you down and prevents you from becoming all that you can be?

Does something keep you from feeling free as a person?

If you have family problems, they don't have to last forever. Seek counseling, even if you have to do it by yourself at first.

If you have an addiction, you can get help. By the grace of God, you can defeat it.

If you have a love for entertainment...gaming, or even Youtube videos...that keeps you from achieving excellence, you don't have to chase that emptiness any longer. Games are fun, if you keep them in the proper perspective.

Regardless of what ties you down, you can remain assured of one fact.

God is stronger than anything that ties you down.

Put the past where it belongs...
IN THE PAST

What does it mean to put something in the past?

The Bible tells us that, when God forgives us, He places our sins as far away from us as the East is from the West.

No matter where you're from, that's pretty far.

There are two different ways in which we have to put the past behind us. There are two different ways in which we have to think like a defensive back.

First, we should remember the expression that holding a grudge is like drinking poison and expecting the other person to die.

Grudges are poisonous.

Hate is poisonous.

There is nothing good about either one.

There are plenty of people who hate others, so that job is already taken. There are also plenty of people who hold grudges...who can't put the past behind them...so that job is taken too.

Two of the top reasons that people don't achieve and enjoy excellence are grudges and self-condemnation. They're both the same, except that one means holding a grudge against others and the other means holding a grudge against yourself.

In short, they're both wrong.

Don't do either one of them.

No matter who you are, you've been forgiven of many things during your life.

If you are having trouble forgiving...if you have a desire to hold a grudge...please know that your desire does not come from God. Please ask Him every single day to relieve you from this weight that you are carrying.

If you have done something bad, for which you cannot forgive yourself, please ask God to remove that from you.

Life can be heavy enough on its own.

Let's try traveling lightly.

Tunnel Vision

WHAT TIES YOU DOWN?

Before you can truly soar, you have to put away the things that tie you down. In many ways, we are all like the circus elephants in that we allow ourselves to remain tied down.

What ties you down?

**Could it be a lack of confidence in yourself?

**Could it be that you listen to the negative people in your life who don't believe you can soar?

**Could it be a weight that you've been unable to shed, like an addiction or unhealthy habit?

**Could it be the friends with whom you choose to hang around?

**Could it be that you just don't want to grow up and accept the responsibilities that often accompany soaring to new heights?

**Could it be that someone in your life is a high achiever, and you don't want to compete?

The reasons could be endless, but the point is that you, right now, with God's help, can transform yourself. The Bible says it best...that we should lay aside the things that bind us:

> "...let us also **lay aside** every weight, and sin which clings so closely, and let us run with endurance the race that is set before us, looking to Jesus, the founder and perfecter of our faith...."

Put down your past. Make a decision for excellence at home, work, school, or on the playing field.

There's no better time than right now.

2013 National Champions

The Final Poll: The Top 25
Public School Division

USA Football Network, Inc.[1]

1. Hoover (Alabama)

2. Allen (Texas)
3. Booker T. Washington (Florida)
4. Northwestern (South Carolina)
5. Jenks (Oklahoma)
6. Mallard Creek (North Carolina)
7. Bellevue (Washington
8. Blue Springs (Missouri)
9. South Jordan (Utah)
10. Eden Prarie (Minnesota)
11. Mountain Plante (Arizona)
12. East Jefferson (Louisiana)
13. Northwestern (South Carolina)
14. Bingham (Utah)
15. Maryville (Tennessee)
16. Centreville (Virginia)
17. Oak Grove (Michigan)
18. Kimberly (Wisconsin)
19. Punahou (Hawaii)
20. Norcross (Georgia)
21. Manatee (Florida)
22. Bowling Green (Kentucky)
23. Derby (Kansas)
24. DeSoto (Texas)
25. McDonough (Maryland)

1
Retrieved from http://www.usahighschoolfootball.com/. January 7, 2014.

Tunnel Vision

Chapter 3

Focus During Adversity

When the Hoover Bucs ran through the tunnel and back onto the field, they once again saw the ugly numbers on the scoreboard: Vestavia 21, Hoover 10.

Josh Niblett accepts the Coach of the Year award for Alabama Class 6A football.

Media and fans across the state, and even in the national media, were suddenly interested in this game. Hoover, the possible national champion, had not lost a game in 2 years or a home game in 4 years.

Fans, alumni, media, and especially their opponents wondered what new strategies would emerge in the second half. They wondered what changes the coaches would make in the game plan. They wondered whether the coaches had thrown out the game plan and devised a new plan of attack.

For Hoover Head Coach Josh Niblett, the plan was simple.

"Keep doing the same thing; just do it better."

Seriously?

"It's never about the other team or what they do," Niblett explained. "Our games are about whether we play to a heightened standard of excellence."

Niblett believes that the entire season depends on that one ideal.

"We just want our destiny as a team to depend on what we do...not what our opponents do, or what someone on the outside does."

So what was the second half game plan to overcome a huge lead by rival Vestavia in the final four of the state playoffs?

"We just had to focus on doing what we do best."

At first that might sound like some expression that all coaches use, but with Niblett, it's different.

Niblett draws inspiration from a man named Harland.

In fact, every football player, every athlete, every business leader, every student, every person in a relationship, and everybody else could learn a lesson from a Harland.

If you're like most people, you will have moments in life when you're ready to give up. Even your friends will tell you that it's time to be realistic and give up. Those moments are painful, and your response to those moments will often define your life.

That's why Harland's story remains so powerful.

Harland had not been successful very often in his life. In fact, he had failed at almost everything he did. He had tried jobs and careers, but nothing seemed to go well for him.

Through the years, Harland had tried more jobs than most people, including the following:

Guess who knocked on

1,009

doors before
succeeding?

     --a farmhand,

     --an army mule-tender,

     --a locomotive fireman,

     --a railroad worker,

     --an aspiring lawyer,

     --an insurance salesman,

     --a ferryboat entrepreneur,

     --a tire salesman,

     --an amateur obstetrician,

     --an (unsuccessful) political candidate,

     --a gas station operator,

     --a motel operator

     --and finally, a restaurateur.

Clearly, Harland was a man who could not hold down a good job for long.

At first, things seemed to go fairly well with the restaurant. Unfortunately, all of that changed for Harland when the news broke that a new interstate highway would be built. Normally, that's good news, but his restaurant would have to be torn down because it was in the path of the new highway.

So, once again, Harland had no job. Everyone seemed to like his cooking, so he decided to find restaurants that would serve his food.

Harland decided to try every restaurant in town, and beyond. He knocked on the door of one near his own place, but they turned him down. He knocked on a second door, but they weren't interested.

Harland then knocked on a third door, followed by a fourth and a fifth.

Josh Niblett (center, in white) enjoys the 2014 Under Armour All-American game with Hoover's All-Americans.
Also pictured are Josh's son Shaw (left), All-American Marlon Humphrey (third from right), and 2014 rising stars Christian Bell (far right), Bradrick Shaw (second from right), and Darrell Williams (third from left).

He had no luck at all.

Harland kept a list of the restaurants he visited to offer a deal to serve his food. The list of five became a list of twenty. That list reached fifty, and a few weeks later, it reached one hundred.

Harland kept knocking on doors, and he kept the list for motivation...and probably to make sure that he didn't waste time by visiting the same restaurant twice.

After more weeks, the list grew to two hundred, and then to five hundred.

Harland didn't give up because he knew the truth. Harland knew that his food was delicious. He knew that the first restaurant to give him a chance would reap great benefits. He also knew that he had the inner strength to keep knocking on restaurant doors until he succeeded.

In other words, Harland knew the question wasn't whether he would succeed; it was WHEN he would succeed.

But he kept knocking, and the list of rejections grew. The list of five hundred became a list of seven hundred, and then ultimately nine hundred.

Finally, the list of restaurants that had rejected Harland reached one thousand.

Then, soon afterward, something changed.

The owner of the 1009th restaurant, amazingly, said yes.

Harland was in business again.

His food was delicious; his chicken recipe was especially great. That 1009th restaurant did so well, that other restaurants suddenly wanted to sell his food too.

Harland began selling his food, especially the chicken, to many restaurants. He kept his chicken recipe a secret, and ultimately opened his own restaurant again.

If the idea of a secret chicken recipe sounds familiar, it should. Harland, better known as Colonel Sanders, founded *Kentucky Fried Chicken*, known these days as *KFC*.

Consider the following questions:

Where would Harland have been if he had listened to those who said he was being delusional when he knocked on over a thousand doors?

Where would Harland have been if he had listened to those who said that the definition of insanity is doing the same thing over and over and expecting a different result?

Where would Harland have been if he did not have the persistence to keep knocking on those days when it seemed futile?

Where would Harland have been if he did not hold strongly to the truths that his food was delicious and that it could succeed if given the right opportunity?

Clearly, this is a story about not giving up. However, the one part of this story that could be easily missed is the fact that Harland, better known as Colonel Sanders, wouldn't give up on doing what he did best: Making incredibly good fried chicken.

Because Colonel Sanders had tried so many other jobs, he finally discovered that his true talents lay in preparing the world's best chicken.

You don't have to be the world's best at anything, but you absolutely can discover the areas where you excel and find enjoyment.

For the Hoover Bucs, attacking Vestavia in the second half meant sticking to their game plan.

Vestavia opened the second half with a quick touchdown, and a 21-10 Rebels' lead suddenly changed to a 28-10 whipping.

For Niblett, the game plan did not change.

"We knew we had a strong game plan. We just had to focus."

They did.

"Our defense," Niblett added, "had to make sure that Vestiavia did not score again."

They didn't.

"Our offense had to just run the ball with power to get first downs and allow us to choose when we could throw. If we did that, we felt we could score enough touchdowns to win."

We did.

"The key is to be yourself," Niblett explained. "Coaches have to do what they do best. We can't worry about what the media or the critics say. Writers have to write what they know. Chefs have to prepare the food that they do best. God has blessed us with different gifts, and we need to become good stewards of those gifts by using them to the best of our ability."

The Honorable John H. Merrill, who knew Niblett through the Fellowship of Christian Athletes long before Niblett was a coach and Merrill was elected to office, believes that authenticity is a key to Niblett's success. "Josh Niblett is considered by many to be the most successful coach in America. It takes a rare person to inherit a great national program like Hoover and elevate it."

Hoover and Vestavia have one of the fiercest and more storied rivalries in all of high school football. On that autumn night, despite facing a seemingly insurmountable Vestavia lead, the Hoover Bucs stuck to their game plan and executed it with the focus that has made them, and their coach, famous.

That focus carried them to the win, and ultimately to the national championship.

That focus is the focus of this book.

That focus is the lesson that Coach Josh Niblett wants you to learn, and to share.

That focus is called TUNNEL VISION.

Tunnel Vision

Chapter 4

Focus
on the Impossible

When they planned the journey, they had no idea that it would change America forever.

It was just a trip, on American roads, but it would change our culture, the way we do business, and the way we travel.

The US Army sent a large convoy across the nation, from Washington DC to San Francisco. They wanted to test their ability to move large numbers of soldiers, weapons, and equipment during wartime conditions. They moved 24 officers and 258 enlisted men, along with the cars, tanks, et al.

How long did it take to travel from Washington to San Francisco?

A day? Two days? An entire week?

Try 62 days.

The year was 1919, and the officers and soldiers had a long trip ahead of them. They drove vehicles, and tried out a new type of weapon called a "tank." Yes, the tank was brand new.

Sereno & Dwight

joined a 62-day drive from Washington, DC to San Francisco, CA.

That journey would one day change the world.

Enter two guys named Sereno and Dwight.

A young officer, Dwight volunteered to lead the convoy. He had volunteered to fight in Europe during World War I, but the Army kept him in the states.

Dwight and his buddy, Major Sereno Brett, quickly learned how difficult cross-country travel could be.

One of the most important people in the convoy was the scout, who drove a day ahead to mark the roads and bridges so the convoy would not get lost.

Even with the scout, the journey was both difficult and dangerous. Many of the bridges could barely support cars; trucks and tanks were out of the question. The Army had to repair and even build bridges along the way. Sometimes, the convoy would cross rivers and creeks by just driving through the water and hoping they would make it.

Many of them didn't.

Several of the vehicles broke down and couldn't be repaired. Stories abound about vehicles being stuck in mud or sand, while still on the roads. One vehicle was actually blown off a cliff while driving. Many of the mechanics in 1919 had been trained to fix horse-drawn wagons, so fixing jeeps, trucks, and tanks was a bit of a stretch.

After 62 days of travel, Sereno, Dwight, and the others in the convoy understood that America was not a nation of great roads.

Why does that story matter to you?

It matters because one of the guys, Dwight, was able to think outside the box. Dwight was able to see things not as they were, but as they could be.

Josh Niblett (center) poses with his parents, John and Brenda, who were the first to teach him how to dream the impossible and see the invisible.

Dwight, a youngster at the time, grew up to become President Dwight D. Eisenhower. During his time in office, President Eisenhower pioneered the US Interstate highway system. He understood that we needed the ability to travel across our vast country, and he saw how it could happen. That's why our interstates are named the Dwight Eisenhower Interstate Highway System.

Coach Josh Niblett lives his life under the theory of seeing the invisible. "One of my favorite motivational speakers is Kevin Elko. Dr. Elko teaches that, to do the impossible, you have to learn to see the invisible.

"One of the biggest mistakes people make is to think the past will repeat itself. That type of thinking robs people of the capacity to change and grow."

When Niblett's dad, John, became the head coach at Demopolis Academy, he inherited a team that had won only one game the year before. All he brought was his mind, his successful system, and a rising eleventh grade son named Josh.

Most people saw the record of the past and presumed that the team couldn't win. John Niblett, the architect of so many other winners, knew better.

"Dad didn't have to call any team meetings at Demopolis Academy when I was there, because I did it for him. We were on the same page. We saw a path to victory and championships, and we had to stick to it."

Did past failures matter at Demopolis Academy? Did losses the year before mean anything to the Nibletts?

Hardly.

Dr. Buddy Gray, minister of Hunter Street Baptist Church and the Niblett family's pastor, served on the committee that interviewed Josh for the vacant Hoover High School Head Football Coach position.
(Photo retrieved from:
https://pastorron7.wordpress.com/tag/buddy-gray/)

In John Niblett's second year as coach, Josh's senior year, Demopolis Academy won the state championship.

They refused to believe that the players and team at Demopolis Academy were limited by the past.

They were right.

John Niblett and his quarterback son implemented an offense much more complicated than most schools ran twenty-five years ago.

"Even in the 1970's, when more teams ran the wishbone or the option out of the I-formation, I ran empty backfields and four wide receiver sets," he added. "In small private schools, we didn't have the athletes that other schools did, so we had to improvise."

In other words, Niblett had to see players doing things they had never tried before. He had to see players at positions they had never attempted to learn.

He had to do the impossible by seeing the invisible.

The sports world is filled with stories of people who succeeded because they refused to settle for the ideas of the past.

Jim was a big guy (especially for a quarterback in the late 1970's), standing 6-foot-3 and weighing 230 pounds. He was offered a football scholarship at Penn State, and dutifully reported for fall practice. During the first practice, the coaches informed him that he would be playing linebacker. Guys his size were linebackers, he was told.

Jim nicely bade the coaches goodbye, and began looking for

another college.

The University of Miami was not a football school until Jim Kelly arrived as a transfer quarterback. Miami's Coach Howard Schnellenberger saw Kelly as the great player he was. As a record setting quarterback, he put the Hurricanes on the map and then led the Buffalo Bills to four Super Bowls en route to a Hall of Fame career.

If Jim had listened to the naysayers, the coaches who told him that he was too thick to be a quarterback, his entire life would have been much different.

Luckily for Magic Johnson, he had coaches who were unafraid to let a 6-foot-9 player become a giant point guard.

Luckily for Cam Newton, he had coaches who had imagination to see a 6-foot-5, 250 pound player become a giant quarterback rather than a tight end or defensive end.

The ability to look beyond the present is something that John Niblett thankfully imparted to his sons. The impact of that gift is unmistakeable.

Dr. Buddy Gray, Senior Pastor at Hunter Street Baptist Church in Hoover, served on the search committee that interviewed Niblett for the position of Hoover's head coach.

"In his interview, Josh was different from the other candidates," Dr. Gray recalled. "He spoke of having a vision for the program and for the integrity with which he would lead the program."

These days, Niblett might call that concept Tunnel Vision.

William Faulkner once described a place by stating that, when you're there, the past isn't only not dead...the past is not even in the past.

Doing the impossible and seeing the invisible both require you to refuse living in the past. Most people don't believe they live in the past, but many do. They think their mistakes, their relationships, and other events will repeat themselves. They believe that they, and others, will never really change.

They are wrong.

People change every day.

Poor students become scholars. People lose large amounts of weight. Others become well conditioned athletes. Recovery groups across the world are examples of people who change because they quit an addiction. Marriages and relationships are saved because people refuse to believe that the past is prologue.

Think back to the story about Dwight and the interstate highway system. Others had expressed an interest in a national road system, but Dwight D. Eisenhower made it happen. Others had wanted to dream of better transportation, but Dwight had lived the experience and understood what was needed.

What can you see that others can't? What is it that you want to be? What standard of excellence would you like to impose on your life?

Have you failed at anything in the past? Are there people who tell you that you can't do something? Are there people who believe that you ARE your past mistakes?

Chances are, those people weren't at Demopolis Academy when the Nibletts turned around a team from one win to the state champions.

That's because the students and fans of Demopolis Academy have seen the Nibletts strive for excellence without regard for what might seem impossible.

That's because the Nibletts can see the invisible...looking past the the things that anyone could see.

That's because the Nibletts have Tunnel Vision.

Tunnel Vision

Chapter 5

Focus on the Foundation

Lawrence was stunned.

In his day, Lawrence of Arabia was one of the most famous people in the world. At the end of World War I, he accompanied several Arab leaders to the Paris Peace Conference of 1919.

While in the City of Lights, he showed his guests all that Paris had to offer...including the Arch de Triumph, the Eiffel Tower, the Louvre.

Josh Niblett accepts the victor's trophy for the Great American Rivalry Series, sponsored by iHish.com.

Although the Arab leaders enjoyed the Parisian sights, one thing above all others amazed them.

They were captivated by running water.

The Arabs, well educated, sophisticated rulers, couldn't get over the idea of turning a faucet and receiving water.

When the day of departure came, Lawrence knocked on the door of the hotel suite occupied by his guests. When he entered, he found them trying to disconnect the faucet from the plumbing.

As you might imagine, he asked why.

The answer was simple: If they could take the faucets to their homeland, all of their water problems would be solved.

As Lawrence quickly explained, the faucet delivers the water but is not the source.

Faucets are wonderful things, but they are not the source of the water.

For Hoover Coach Josh Niblett, a key to his success is understanding its source. That means understanding the foundation of his life.

There is never any doubt about either his foundation or his purpose.

"My purpose in life is to serve and glorify God," he explained. "We're told to seek first the kingdom of God, and all these things shall be added unto us. If I seek to honor God first in my life, the other things will fall in line."

So how do you do it?

How do you make God the foundation for your life? Plenty of people attend church, and many people claim to follow God. How is it, though, that we can make God our actual foundation?

One way to do it is by following these three simple, and easy steps that will help keep you mindful, on a daily basis, of who is in charge and who is your sustainer.

Foundation for
Success

Give Credit

For Niblett, the easiest part of success is giving credit for it.

"Why am I where I am today? First, it's my relationship with my Lord & Savior, Jesus Christ. I wake up every morning grateful for this opportunity, even though it's not because of anything I've done."

The next for Niblett is simple: If your success is not because of anything you have done, then how do you reply when people praise you for your success?

"I know the success is not my own," he added. "That's why, when people tell me congratulations, I say 'To God be the glory.' That has to be the cornerstone if you're really successful."

Niblett is quick to add that success on the field doesn't mean success all the time. "That doesn't mean everything is perfect, or that I don't go through trials and tribulations. But I do think relationships are a key to living a life of significance. It's not about survival or success."

That begs the question of what success really means. As with any question about his faith or success, the coach did not hesitate to answer.

"Life is about relationships, beginning with our relationship with God. I've always had great respect for the relationships I've had with people.

"Life boils down to how many relationships you can impact and how many things you can learn. One great thing about being a coach is the number of people, in the daily path of life, whom I can possibly impact."

According to Niblett, the key part of success is understanding the identity of its author. "That makes it easy to give credit for success and to remain thankful," he added.

That brings us to the second foundation for success, which is:

Foundation for
Success
Give Thanks

Outside the massive building, everything is dark except for the headlights of the approaching car. It's 3:30 a.m., and the gentleman who parked the solitary car knows that he'll be alone in his office for the next few hours.

That's exactly the way he likes it.

Dr. Buddy Gray is the senior pastor at Hoover's Hunter Street Baptist Church, one of the strongest and most successful churches in the state and beyond. Hunter Street transitioned under Dr. Gray to a family of thousands seeking to impact Hoover for God's glory. On this Sunday morning, like all Sunday mornings, Gray arrives long before sunrise to prepare.

Is his message not ready?

Actually, it's not that type of preparation. His messages are already prepared, but Gray arrives early to prepare his heart.

"I thank God for the day, and treat it as if it's my last Sunday at Hunter Street. Every week I tell God that I understand there any many out there who can do this better than I. I'm just so grateful for the opportunity to serve God and show overflowing gratitude to Him each week."

Who else shows up at the office, at 3 a.m., out of gratitude for their career and calling?

Most of us probably don't know anyone who does that.

Who else renews their gratitude each week?

Look no farther than Josh Niblett.

Niblett and Gray have a lot in common. They are members of the same church, where Gray is the pastor and Niblett one of its most well known members. Both have a rich history with the Hoover schools, with Niblett winning championships there in part because Gray served on the committee that recommended him for the job.

Most of all, their greatest commonality just might be gratitude.

"I'm so grateful to be the Head Coach of Hoover High School and to help kids become men," he said proudly. "I get to do this every day, and I realize what an incredible opportunity it is."

Niblett, like his pastor Gray, believes that gratitude spurs excellence. "If you're truly grateful for a tremendous opportunity, you'll work even harder to show your gratitude. I tell my players that they have been blessed with good health, a great community, and a championship tradition at Hoover."

Foundation for Success

Give Up Control

On a hot August day, the kids were excited. After all, it was the first day of the school year. For the kids in one class, it was the first day of the first grade. During the first hour, as the teacher was helping the kids become comfortable on their first day, she asked if any student could name the seasons of the year.

"I can," one little boy called out.

The teacher asked him to say his name for the class, and then gently asked him how many seasons there are.

"Three," he replied boldly.

She smiled and nodded as only a first grade teacher could, and then asked if maybe he meant to say that there were four seasons.

He confidently repeated that there are three seasons in the year.

She decided to let him answer anyway, so she asked him to name the seasons of the year.

He smiled and stated for the entire class to hear: "There are three seasons...baseball season, football season, and basketball season."

That child didn't have all the answers, but he gave everything he had to the class in terms of a first grader's knowledge.

As we grow, we realize that we truly don't have all the answers (at least most of us realize that). However, that is not a bad thing. Understanding that we don't have all the answers can make us more open to learning and wisdom from others. Most importantly, it can open our eyes to the power of God.

According to Josh Niblett, there is great freedom in asking God for direction each day.

He believes that giving up that control is a daily event. "How do you know if God's really sending you down that road...having faith & trust in Him...waking up every day and saying: 'Here I am...I'm ready to go, but I need you to show me what direction you want me to go.'

"You've got to follow Him every day. You're not gonna be perfect. We've all sinned and fallen short of the glory of God, but we've got a cornerstone, and that cornerstone is what everything is built off of."

Dr. Gray believes that Niblett's success, built on a strong foundation, prevents the stumbles that have plagued so many others. "One great thing about Josh is the way he has handled his success. When people are given a platform, a couple of bad things can happen. They might begin to think that they did it all themselves, or they may be attacked. There are many different ways that people can be attacked, and so many people love to see public figures fall."

For Niblett, focusing on his foundation keeps him grounded, humble, and realistic. That focus requires unwavering attention.

That focus requires Tunnel Vision.

Tunnel Vision

Chapter 6

Focus on the Home Team

Walking into the Niblett home is at first nothing unusual. To the right sits a small study. To the left...a living room that leads into the family dining room.

At the head of the dining room, prominently centered on the wall, hangs a large, framed portrait-sized photograph. As with many portraits, the photo captures loved ones posing and looking their best.

Because the photo is large, framed, and located alone on the dining room wall, it is clearly treasured.

Unlike many photos, this one reveals much about the Niblett family. It explains a great deal about their teamwork as a family, their ministry, their mission, and their quest to raise children who look outward rather than focusing solely on themselves.

How can a large family photo, hanging on a wall, reveal so much?

The family photo, given the most prominent place in the Niblett home, features the senior football players, in full uniform, from the current team.

Many people speak of reaching out to others. Many people will say they want their kids to look beyond their own lives. For Josh and Karon Niblett, along with their kids Shaw (15), Harper (12), and Sky (9), ministry is much more than something other people do; it's a family commitment.

Josh and Karon Niblett are partners in family, ministry, and life. They open their home each week to the Hoover Bucs, and have seen lives change over the years.

Simply put, the family is a team. Like many dads with demanding jobs, Josh works hard to make sure he attends as many of his kids' events as possible. Unlike many dads, his kids can also come join him on the field as he does his job.

Karon's life includes countless practices, games, and family dinners...as do the lives of many families. For her, the games also include her husband and brother-in-law. For her, family dinners on Wednesdays

52

also include 50 to 60 football players in their home.

For Karon, as with Josh, the task is to reconcile giving their children an ordinary family life with the goal of providing an extraordinary life. The goal is to provide everything they need while teaching them to look beyond their needs.

How, one might ask, do the Nibletts pull it off? How can they raise their kids, engage fully with their players, serve the roles in Hoover required of the head coach's family, and maintain their sanity?

One word: FOCUS.

Dr. Buddy Gray, the Niblett family's pastor, believes the commitment to family helps define Josh Niblett and his career. "Thankfully, Josh is not one of those people who will sacrifice his family for success. Josh understands the importance of family, and he and Karon are doing a great job raising their kids."

> *"The Nibletts greatly help their children by teaching them to enjoy focusing on others rather than on their own entertainment."*
> *---Dr. Jane N. Geiger family therapist*

Gray also believes that authenticity is a major part of their ministry. "You see all that energy and it's easy to wonder, or at least hope, that it's the real thing. I've seen too many others that appear to be one thing and are not. I have had the privilege of getting to know and learn about their family beyond just them, and I know the type of people they come from. They are the real thing."

Another way to see their authenticity is to visit their home the week of their rivalry game. In Hoover, walking into the Niblett home the week of the Vestavia game is like going to the Saban or Malzahn home the week of the Iron Bowl. It would be like going to Urban Meyer's home the week of the Michigan game.

According to Dr. Jane N. Geiger, a therapist and founder & CEO of Grace Ministries, leading children to look beyond their own entertainment is one of the most important parts of parenting. "So many make everything about their children. The Nibletts greatly help their children by teaching them to enjoy focusing on others rather than their own entertainment."

In the Niblett's den, Josh leads a group of roughly 50 players in his off-campus Bible study.

It's no small irony that the players, gathered the week they face Coach Buddy Anderson's rival Vestavia team, are together on this night in part because of Anderson himself.

"The group meetings began when I was a graduate assistant coach at Jacksonville State. That was easy. But when I became the head coach at Oneonta, and I wanted to start a group there, I wasn't sure whether it would violate the law or become anything inappropriate."

The coach smiled. "I learned that Vestavia Head Coach Buddy Anderson held Bible studies for players in his home. Buddy Anderson was my cover; his ministry empowered me to continue the ministry I had begun at J.S.U."

As Anderson becomes Alabama's all-time winningest high school football coach in 2014, it's fitting that he is both the father of Vestavia's Bible study ministry and basically the grandfather of his rival Hoover's ministry.

Out of respect to the Hoover schools and the laws of the land, Niblett carefully separates his Bible studies and all faith related activities from his job. "If I were to overstep my authority and violate the law, it would hurt everything we stand for...on and off the field. We teach the kids to work hard and play by the rules, so we will do that in our own lives."

But in the Niblett home, all the players are welcomed to show up each Wednesday evening for Bible study and dinner.

The kids are remarkably attentive. Niblett speaks of excellence, as sons to their parents, in relationships, and in their studies.

For a while, football is not even mentioned.

"Have you ever been in love?"

The question provoked laughter, looks around the room, and even some jocular finger pointing.

The coach explains that the joy of accepting Christ is a lot like the joy of falling in love, except the joy of Jesus is permanent. He tells one of his favorite stories...of the way he met his wife.

After having heard the story in a private lunch, the joy with which he described Karon in both accounts was striking. The man clearly enjoys talking about his bride.

The story itself, as he tells it, is entertaining.

"I was a graduate assistant at Jacksonville State," he began. "A local minister did a devotion for the team, and I was impressed. I felt led to visit that minister's church."

As a good speaker, Niblett naturally builds his body language and voice inflection as he approaches the crescendo of the story.

"I saw this red haired girl in the choir, and I had to meet her. The next day, I called the church and asked to speak to the choir director. I asked him who the redhead was in the choir, and if he could put me in touch with her. He laughed and said there were two redheads in the choir; which one did I want to meet?"

The players laughed.

"I told him I would trust that he could figure out which redhead I wanted to meet."

The players laughed again.

"The choir director guessed correctly, and called Karon to ask her if she would be willing to speak with me. The rest is history."

That redhead has been Josh's wife, partner, and best friend as they have spent their lives building together. Karon smiles as

The Nibletts, pictured on Easter Sunday, 2014, teach their children the value and joy of ministry each week by hosting dozens of Hoover Bucs players in their homes. Pictured, L-R, are..(front row): Harper, Sky ; (middle row) Karon, Shaw; (back row) Josh.

broadly as her husband when asked about their life together. "We've built a beautiful family together," she explained. "Our entire family has helped Josh build his career. Even more important than football, though, is the ministry that we've built through the years. So many young people have accepted Christ in this home, and in our homes in Oxford and Oneonta. For both of us, it's one of life's greatest joys."

For Heather Niblett, Josh's little sister, the relationship between Karon and Josh is no surprise. "Josh loves Karon and is a great role model of how to treat a lady."

Heather laughed as she decided to tell a story on her brother. "When I was in high school, I was always disappointed at how few dates I had. After Bob and I got married, Josh confessed that he had told all his teammates, in no uncertain terms, that none of them were allowed to ask me out. He was protective because he loves me."

The Wednesday night Bible study continued with prayer for the kids who were present, those who weren't, and especially for their injured teammates. As Karon readied the meal, Josh concluded the lesson. He referenced his pupils as sons, students, brothers, and even boyfriends. The lesson, based on scripture, involved the joy of the Lord.

Coach Wayne Wood, who has dutifully served Hoover for decades, believes Josh Niblett is one of the great coaches in high school football.

Afterward, the players enjoyed pizza while talking to each other, enjoying video games with the Niblett kids, playing ping pong downstairs, or chatting with either the Nibletts or the Kings, who have come to help.

If anyone feels invested in the Hoover football program, it's the King family.

Their son Daniel, a special-needs child, grew into adulthood and dearly loves football. One local college, with a caring coach, gave their son his first opportunity, a volunteer position on the staff. Daniel loved all of his time with the college football program.

Strangely enough, when a new head coach was hired at that college, he considered Daniel to be a distraction and terminated the position.

Daniel, and his parents, were greatly surprised and deeply disappointed. "Daniel did a good job and the players loved him, so we were sad for him," Jenise King recalled. "We understand that sometimes a public image is different from the way people treat others privately, but that didn't make it any easier for Daniel."

Enter the Niblett family.

During that same period of time, Josh Niblett was hired as the Hoover Head Coach. When he learned the story of Daniel, a Hoover alumnus, Niblett offered him a position on the staff.

Challenged and motivated, Daniel quickly excelled in his new position.

Today, Daniel King serves as the Motivational Coach of the national champion Hoover Bucs.

56

"We'll always be indebted to Josh and Karon," Mr. King added. "They have reached out to Daniel, included him with the players and staff, and challenged him to give all he has for the team."

Not surprisingly, the Kings invoke many of the same words to describe the Nibletts that are used by their pastor, former players and parents of players, and people who know them.

"The Nibletts are good people, and they are real people. What you see is what you get. They don't claim religion as a PR move; they have a real relationship with God. They don't just say they love their players; they treat them like family."

"The key to treating people like family is accepting them," Josh Niblett opined. "Our players come from different types of families, and they come from different types of circumstances. They also come with different types of belief systems. But that doesn't matter; they're all welcomed here because we love them the way they are."

> *"Our children have learned at an early age to look beyond themselves," she added. "They share their home, their time, their ping pong table, and their video games with these high school students. They do it every week, so thankfully the idea of sharing has become part of their lives."*
>
> *---Karon Niblett*

According to Karon Niblett, the Wednesday ministry has been a great way to teach their children. "Our children have learned at an early age to look beyond themselves," she added. "They share their home, their time, their ping pong table, and their video games with these high school students. They do it every week, so thankfully the idea of sharing has become part of their lives. Josh and I pray that they will always share what they have with others."

Coach Wayne Woods, who has coached in the Hoover program and authored a book on the subject, believes Niblett's concern for every part of his players' lives is the secret to his success.

"That's one way in which Niblett reminds me of (Berry) Coach Bob Finley," Woods remarked. "Josh Niblett really cares how they connect to God, how they relate to their families, and how well they perform as students."

Dr. Buddy Gray recalls fondly that Niblett made the players a priority in his life before he ever met them. As a member of the committee that interviewed Niblett, he heard the coach say something unforgettable.

"Josh said matter-of-factly that if he comes to Hoover they would win big, but that it's not about that. Josh had faith...complete biblical faith... that they would enjoy success on the football field, but that they would enjoy much greater success OFF the field. I'll never forget hearing that."

Speaking of unforgettable, the benefits received by the Niblett family outweigh all the costs and efforts required by their outreach. "We've had so many students give their lives to Christ over the years," Karon Niblett recalled with a smile. "That's the most important thing of all. If God uses our family to make an eternal impact, then it's the best investment we could make with our time, and it's the best lesson we can teach our children."

And that, as Niblett will say, makes all the focus worthwhile.

Tunnel Vision

Chapter 7

Focus on the Path

Josh Niblett faced a life changing decision.

After two years at the University of Southern Mississippi, he believed it was time to transfer to another college.

If he believed he had been given the full opportunity to compete for the starting job, he would have stayed.

Josh Niblett (left) introduces his sons Shaw (inside left) and Sky (right) to Alabama Head Coach Nick Saban (red shirt). An alumnus of Alabama, Niblett played for the Crimson Tide after leaving a full scholarship at Southern Miss to become a non-scholarship walk-on in Tuscaloosa.

Since that was not the case, he prepared to choose the place he would spend the rest of his college years.

Unlike many players, he had choices. Those options, however, were complicated.

As a high school senior, Josh was blessed with a number of options and scholarship offers. He anticipated that many of those offers would be renewed.

Two offers, however, stood out above the rest. They were both close to his heart, but could not have been more dissimilar.

Harding University, in Arkansas, featured a star quarterback who had just graduated and would serve as a graduate assistant coach helping teach the quarterbacks. That star quarterback, who was named all-conference, was none other than Josh's older brother Tad.

The idea of transferring to Harding and being coached by his big brother was priceless. Despite being hundreds of miles apart, in the days before social media, the two brothers remained the closest of friends. They often talked of coaching together one day, and this could be the beginning of that journey.

On Friday nights, while other kids went out and socialized, Tad and Josh went home with their dad and broke down game films. Joining forces on the college level would merely be going back to the future for the Niblett boys.

Harding University also brought the type of academic and athletic respect that could help Josh become everything that his potential represented. He knew the campus well already, having visited many times. Having big brother around would make everything much easier than it might be for a typical transfer student.

"Playing college ball with my big brother coaching me was an idea I really liked," Josh said with a grin. "We've always been really close, and we would have made a great team even back then."

Tad Niblett agreed. "I recruited Josh, and the coaches wanted him too. As a grad assistant, I would be doing much of the quarterback coaching. We both liked the idea and talked about it a lot."

There was, however, one thing that might pull Josh in a different direction. In fact, it just might be the only thing that could keep him from playing for his big brother on the college level.

About an hour-long drive northward from Josh's high school alma mater in Demopolis, stood the one object that had fascinated Josh since childhood. That object was both a pathway and its own destination. That object, and everything it represented, proved to be irresistible.

That object was the tunnel.

Bryant Denny Stadium opened in 1929, and since the first kickoff, kids and their parents have cheered as they watched countless All-American players, great coaches, and championship teams run through the tunnel out onto the famed field.

One of those kids was Josh Niblett.

As he sat in his dorm room in Hattiesburg, Mississippi, it was not the first time he seriously considered running through that tunnel in Tuscaloosa.

During his senior year of high school, he was being recruited by the Alabama Crimson Tide. On a wintery Friday, the Niblett family received a call from one of the Tide's assistant coaches. They had narrowed their quarterback search to Josh, and a quarterback from Cedartown, Georgia. The coaching staff had already offered the other quarterback, but they suspected he would go elsewhere. If so, then Josh would get that scholarship offer.

Josh spent much of that weekend harboring thoughts of running through the Bryant Denny tunnel with a flood of crimson jerseys on championship teams.

Josh's dad remembered the conversations vividly. "On that Friday, the Alabama coach believed he would be offering that scholarship to Josh in the next few days," he recalled. "We thought he would be suiting up for Alabama in a few months."

All of that changed on the following Monday, when the coach called back with the news that the other quarterback accepted the Crimson Tide's scholarship offer.

Now, once again, the thought of joining the grand Alabama tradition became real, but under vastly different circumstances. Rather than the coaches recruiting him with a scholarship opportunity, Josh would ask the coaches if he could join the team as a non-scholarship player (called a "walk-on").

"If I walked on at Alabama, I would be leaving a full scholarship at Southern Miss," Josh explained. "Some people might think it wasn't a wise thing to do."

Josh's dad was more direct. "Josh wanted to run through that tunnel, in Bryant Denny Stadium, wearing that crimson uniform. One thing Josh and Tad have in common is that when they make up their minds about something, it's hard to derail either one of them."

Unfortunately for Josh, he wasn't the only person who was hard to derail. He knew Alabama was loaded with good players, and that he would have to sit out the 1992 season as a transfer student before becoming eligible to play the next season.

Sitting out the year was made more complicated because of the Alabama roster. Alabama had just finished the 1991 season with a top-five ranking and an 11-1 record with young quarterbacks on the team.

At Southern Miss, he was a quarterback on scholarship. At Alabama, he would have no scholarship and might not even be a quarterback. He might not ever see the field during a real game. Would he succeed?

He might not ever run through that tunnel.

There were no guarantees, and the risks were plentiful.

At that point, Josh turned to words he has followed since childhood. Josh had been taught the Bible verse about hiding God's word in our hearts, and the time had come to search his heart for those words. For him, there was no doubt which words to follow.

Brenda Niblett, his mother, still smiles when asked about the moment when he found those words.

Josh prepares to throw out the first pitch at a Birmingham Barons game in the Hoover Met. Sky Niblett accompanied his dad.

"Josh was about six years old," she recalled. "He opened my Bible, and found a verse I had marked. He decided at that moment that the verse, Joshua 1:9, would become his life verse. As he faced a major life decision, Josh's favorite verse spoke volumes:

> *[9] Have I not commanded you? Be strong and courageous. Do not be frightened, and do not be dismayed, for the Lord your God is with you wherever you go."*

Those risks, and the enormity of the challenge, proved irresistible. Josh chose to follow the verse from the book of Joshua, and to be neither frightened nor dismayed.

63

"He chose Alabama," Tad added, "because he was attracted to that challenge."

Roger Schultz, an All-SEC player and later grad assistant at the University of Alabama, saw the Niblett work ethic and knew Josh was headed for success through excellence.

So, Josh gave up his full scholarship, transferred to the University of Alabama, and started all over.

He was a quarterback, and he had almost always been a quarterback growing up. He led his dad's team at Demopolis Academy to the state championship. He was All-State in three different sports. He had many scholarship offers to play quarterback in college. He had been drafted by the Chicago White Sox as a baseball player, but turned it down to be a college quarterback.

In one day, all of that changed.

Now he was at mighty Alabama, and he spent the 1992 season as the quarterback... of the scout team. Each day, in practice, Josh would lead the scout team offense against the number one defense in the nation, and one of the greatest in the history of college football.

The 1992 Alabama team won the national championship, with Josh leading the way in preparing the defense for the team they would face each week.

The next year, 1993, brought his chance to hit the field after sitting out the mandatory season as a transfer student. After all of those years and all that success as a quarterback, the coaches immediately moved him to defensive back.

If you've ever heard of NFL players Sam Shade, Antonia Langham, and Willie Gaston, they were defensive backs ahead of him on the roster at Alabama. It was as bad as the quarterback position, and perhaps worse because Josh had not played defensive back in college.

Josh was ultimately moved back to the offensive side of the ball, but not at his coveted position of quarterback. The coaches decided to try Josh at fullback.

In some offenses, the fullback could be an exciting position.

64

In the 1980's and 90's, the San Franciso 49ers used fullback Tom Rathman as an outstanding receiver on their many Super Bowl teams. When Josh was a kid, the Atlanta Falcons made fullback William Andrews one of the best players in the game. Ten years earlier, Alabama's own fullback Ricky Moore was a star for Bear Bryant and Ray Perkins.

But for Alabama in the early 90's, under Head Coach Gene Stallings, the fullback was used like another offensive lineman most of the time. With rare exceptions, the fullback was a blocker.

There was no glamour. There were few times to carry the ball. Catching a pass was almost out of the question, especially for a walk-on, backup fullback.

The Nibletts celebrate, as a family, at the team bus after the 2012 state championship victory.

To make matters worse, Josh had to sit out the 1992 season as a transfer. That happened to be the year that Alabama won the national championship with a thrilling, improbable 34-13 blowout of the Miami Hurricanes.

For many people, giving up the scholarship, giving up the chance to play quarterback, giving up the notoriety for anonymity, and watching his teammates win the national championship would have been disheartening.

Josh, however, was uninhibited as he pursued excellence.

"Josh always had his eyes on his goals," his dad explained. "He stared directly at his dreams and his goals, and never let anything get in his way. That's why he thrived at Alabama, despite the odds."

One Alabama player who did not toil in anonymity was All-SEC center Roger Schultz. Always a media favorite for interviews, he was, and still is, one of the all-time fan favorites among Crimson Tide fans.

Although Josh Niblett was an unknown walk-on, nobody had to tell Roger Schultz who he was.

"Most college football players don't even know what they're going to do the next Friday night," Schultz said with a chuckle. "None of us thought that far ahead. We might say we want to play in the NFL or something like that, but we really didn't have any plans.

"Josh, on the other hand, was the exception to the rule. He always knew exactly where he was headed. He was farsighted in ways that most other college kids were not."

Josh Niblett confers with a referee during his Hoover Bucs' national championship march of 2013. The season also ended with the second straight undefeated state championship team, and a 30-game winning streak.

John Niblett agreed. "Josh was All-SEC academically each year he was at Alabama. He worked hard, and he studied hard. He just kept his eyes focused on his goals."

Thankfully, Josh had a support system in place in Tuscaloosa. His sister, Heather, was also a student in Tuscaloosa. They lived two doors down from each other in the same apartment complex.

"Josh was always good about inviting me to his FCA (Fellowship of Christian Athletes) meetings at Coach Randy Ross's home," Heather recalled fondly. "Those meetings were always so meaningful to us both, and helped us grow spiritually."

The groups also provided a strong network for Josh as he transitioned into a new city, a new team, a new school, and a new role as an anonymous walk-on.

Finally, after more than a year of waiting, Alabama hit the field in the fall of 1993 as the reigning national champions.

When they ran through that tunnel, Josh was part of the team... sprinting onto the field in a crimson jersey.

He had finally reached his goal.

But there was more to come.

The odds were squarely against walk-ons breaking through for playing time on a team laden with future NFL talent. For Josh, that only presented another challenge.

His dad remembers the next steps fondly. "When Josh finally got to run through that tunnel, he became hungry for more. Then, he became hungry for seriously good playing time. That's what happens when you strive for excellence; the goals are met, and you become hungry for the next challenge."

Josh worked hard to be ready when the next opportunity came. "I had to be ready. We always tell our backup players at Hoover that you have to remain ready at all times, because your moment could come when you least expect it."

During Hoover's march to the national championship, an injury forced them to start their backup quarterback against Hillcrest. Thankfully, he was an experienced and talented player. That meant, however, that the third-string player, a tenth grader, now became the backup and had to be ready.

On the third play from scrimmage, the quarterback was injured. Suddenly, the sophomore who was third-string the week before was the number one guy.

Josh smiles when remembering that moment against Hillcrest. "Suddenly," he added, "The backup players realized we weren't kidding when we said you have to be ready. Our tenth grade, third-string player comes in, plays the toughest position in sports for the number one team in the state, and plays admirably. That was his moment."

Josh's own moment came in an Alabama game against Vanderbilt. That season, the Crimson Tide was plagued by injuries. During the game in Nashville, Coach Stallings wondered aloud who they could send in to block for their running plays. Josh happened to be standing near Stallings on the sidelines, though one didn't have to be nearby to hear the coach during games. Stallings, who could be a great grandfatherly figure during public speeches and dealing with the handicapped, expressed himself more provincially during games.

"I can do it!" Stallings looked at the walk-on who had brazenly proclaimed that he could make the blocks from the fullback position. Maybe it was the timing. Maybe it was the boldness of the walk-on. Maybe it was the knowledge that Josh had already played college ball elsewhere. Maybe it was a combination of them all.

Josh Niblett (left) worked hard and spoke up at a crucial time as a player for Alabama Crimson Tide Coach Gene Stallings (right).

Stallings sent Niblett into the game against an SEC opponent. Niblett threw his blocks, and made his assignments happen. Alabama scored on that drive, and Niblett was rewarded with more playing time.

Josh had taken a colossal risk by leaving behind a scholarship, the quarterback position, and a prominent place on his team.

The risk paid off.

During the second season after he transferred, Josh was featured in *The Tuscaloosa News* as Alabama prepared to play Southern Miss in Tuscaloosa. The article, published on October 29, 1993, gave the readers a glimpse into his character. His competitiveness showed, as he said he had been waiting to play them for two seasons. He also stated that he hoped to gain ten pounds from his then-weight of 219 pounds, because the coaches had moved him from fullback to tight end. Rather than complaining about his move from quarterback, Josh wanted to change his weight in order to play the position at which he was needed.

That attitude became his signature, and the means through which he gained the respect of players, coaches, and opponents ever since.

When he graduated, he entered the coaching world armed with tools for success. He had learned in two different major college programs. He had learned more than one college offense, and how great defenses prepared for them. His time with the defensive backs, under Stallings and Coach Bill Oliver, brought lessons from two Hall of Fame caliber coaches.

His years as an anonymous walk-on taught him respect for the players, like himself, who fight and scratch every day with no promise of running through that tunnel, much less playing in a game.

"I strongly believed that God called me to transfer to Tuscaloosa," Niblett explained. "I didn't know what he had in store for me, but looking back, the Lord teed up so many developments, through the years at Alabama, that taught me lessons we routinely use today at Hoover.

"In my heart, I wake up asking God each day to direct me. I ask HIm what He wants me to do that day. Do I make mistakes? Of course I do. Do I sometimes steer in the wrong direction? You bet. But the important thing is that I seek each day to follow God's will.

"I don't follow God because I'm anything special. It's the opposite; I'm special only because I'm His child.

"As long as I seek His will each day of my life and live according to His purpose, I'll be successful."

Tunnel Vision

Chapter 8

Focus

on the Game Plan

For someone who has played high school sports, attended many college practices, and coached youth sports, watching the Hoover Bucs practice is a joy.

The enthusiasm of athletes, the expectation of success, and the precision of a military unit make a great combination to watch.

The quarterbacks don't just take turns executing passing plays; they run them at the same time while standing no more than six to eight feet from each other. At the same time, two quarterbacks will take a five-step drop, then fire a pass to a receiver on the right side of the field. The two receivers will be running similar routes, but one will run it 15 yards out, and the other only half that far.

> *"Coach Niblett brings an emphasis on everything involving excellence. In the classroom with our studies, we were taught excellence. With the way we dress, treating everyone with respect, and every other way imaginable, we were challenged for excellence."*
> *---Landry Tullo, linebacker*
> *Delta State University*

Meanwhile, the fullbacks practice faking a block, then running a swing route out of the backfield. Josh Niblett, a former All-State quarterback himself, takes over the drills and throws the passes to the fullbacks. Over and over and over, they fake the blocks, run the routes exactly as taught, then haul in the passes. They run first to the right side of the field, and then to the left. Niblett intentionally throws some balls over the outside shoulder of the receivers and some over the inside.

Elsewhere, the WE-fense is practicing.

You've heard of offense and defense, and in Hoover, the WE-fense is the special teams (the kickoff, kicking and punting parts of the game).

For the Hoover Bucs, the WE-fense is not just a task to be checked off the list. Special teams drills are practiced with the same ferocity as any other part of the game.

On this day, under ominously cloudy skies, the WE-fense practices the gunners, who are the guys in punt return coverage who line up on the outside and usually arrive first to tackle the punt returner.

The gunners practiced getting a quick start down the field, eluding the defensive backs assigned to block them, and tackling the punt returner.

At the same time, the defensive backs get plenty of simulated game repetitions as they try to cover and ultimately block Hoover's best gunners.

The punters get plenty of reps, as each fights to be Hoover's new punter. The punter from last season's team, Tuck Borie, is unavailable because he has already enrolled at the University of Alabama and is competing to be the Crimson Tide's punter.

Likewise, Hoover is also breaking in a new punt returner. Last year's punt returner was not only fast, but dubbed one of the fastest people in the world after winning track events in America and Europe. Marlon Humphrey was also a consensus All-American. When fall practice rolls around, he will join the punter in an Alabama uniform.

> *"Coach Niblett is truly a man of God, and an all-around great guy. He backs up what we teach at home, and he wants to take them to the next level of success in all areas of life."*
>
> *---Robert Horn*
> *Hoover football parent*

How will Hoover replace these great players?

They began the last season having to replace their quarterback, both safeties, and several excellent starters from an undefeated state championship team. They responded by winning the national championship.

"It's just like college ball in that we have to replace great players every year, but that's the nature of the game," Niblett explained. "One of the joys of coaching is preparing young players to step up and assume leadership roles on and off the field."

For Niblett, it's all about preparation.

His brother Tad agrees. "There's a reason that Josh and I spent our Friday nights breaking down game film with our dad," he said with a chuckle. "Who else does that during their teenage years? We enjoy the game, and we all enjoy preparing ourselves and the team. We want to have beaten the other teams in many ways before the game starts."

Josh nods at the thought. "I like to think that no one will outwork us. Ever. Our goal is to outwork and outprepare every opponent."

For Niblett, the level of preparation is for both games and life. "We want our kids to learn, at an early age, the value of preparation."

For those players, the lessons resonate long after the playing days at

Hoover have ended. Landry Tullo is a linebacker at Delta State University and a Hoover Bucs alumnus. "First, Coach Niblett brings an emphasis on everything involving excellence. In the classroom with our studies, we were taught excellence. With the way we dress, treating everyone with respect, and every other way imaginable, we were challenged for excellence. I love his practice tempo, his view of special teams, and his attention to detail. I was prepared for all of that when I got to college."

Calen Campbell, a running back at Jacksonville State University, is also grateful for the preparation. "Coach Niblett did a great job of preparing us. They don't call it Hoover U for nothing," he said with a grin. "Coach Niblett made sure we were prepared for college, on and off the field. He gave us a college feel...in the locker room and even in the weight room. Jacksonville State practices at a fast temp, but it's the same tempo we had at Hoover so I was ready.

"Also, just in leaving for college and starting to become a man, I felt like Coach Niblett prepared us to handle all of our stuff like men."

Josh Niblett leaves the team bus with his son, Sky.

Robert Horn knows a thing or two about football, and about preparation. As a small business owner of Affordable Lawn & Chem, he has to prepare well every day in order to pay employees and succeed. As a former player at Birmingham's Ensley High School, Horn was a teammate of Cornelius Bennett, a Hall of Fame linebacker who was Alabama's first three-time All-American and won the Lombardi Award.

As the parent of a Hoover Bucs rising senior lineman, Alex, Robert Horn is grateful for Josh Niblett and the job he has done. "Their culture is second to none," Horn explained. "Coach Niblett is truly a man of God, and an all-around great guy. He backs up what we teach at home, and he wants to take them to the next level of success in all areas of life."

On a crisp, cold January afternoon, over 600 people gathered for the annual Hoover Bucs football banquet. All the players and coaches were joined by parents, boosters, fans, city officials, a leader in the Alabama House of Representatives, and media.

The Nibletts support Hoover Bucs players by traveling to the 2013 Semper Fi All-American game.

It was a grand event. The day brought videos, speakers, awards, the unveiling of *BETTER*, (the book about Hoover's championship season and rich history), and remarks by and about players.

Finally, after everything and everyone else were finished, Head Coach Josh Niblett rose to speak. He didn't speak off the cuff, and he didn't pull out a sheet of notes from the inside of his light cotton suit pocket.

Instead, he brought a notebook.

A notebook?

That's right. Josh Niblett brought a notebook. He was determined to recognize and honor each senior specifically rather than with mere platitudes. He honored each coach, and so many others who contributed mightily to the success of the program. He spoke to inspire, to honor, to celebrate, and to challenge for the future.

He neither used the notebook as a crutch nor let it inhibit his delivery. He achieved every single goal of the speech...in spades. He told a hilarious story about his son during a road trip. He honored both his nuclear family and the family that is his team.

"Coach Niblett did a great job, and kept a large crowd riveted," Dr. Jane N. Geiger observed. "He was determined not to leave anyone out, and he made that notebook work to his advantage."

Finally, he made it abundantly clear that his focus, his aspirations, and his foundation began with his God. He would not let 600 people leave the room without knowing that about him. He was not overbearing or

74

intrusive, but he was absolutely unwavering.

That desire to prepare, and reveal God as the source of goodness, is the explanation for his success. It's also the result of his tunnel vision focus on excellence.

"I still remember the first sermon Josh ever delivered," John Niblett recalled. "The theme was that God's delays are not God's denials. I was so proud of him for boldly proclaiming the gospel."

That's something that both John and Josh do regularly. One church invited Josh to speak, and after accepting, a scheduling change meant that he was unable to go. Rather than just canceling, Josh called his dad and asked him to deliver the message.

John did such a great job, and was so well received, that the church asked John to become their pastor.

"God uses Josh in so many ways, including introducing me to a church that I now love and serve," John added. "It's amazing what God will do when you listen and make yourself available."

Josh needed a break. He needed a fresh start. He needed recalibrating.

The last few days had been even colder than the December weather outside. Josh wasn't depressed, but he was down. His Hoover Bucs had just lost the Alabama State Championship game by one point...for the second year in a row. All that work...all that success...all those wins...only to lose two years in a row by one point each.

For the last couple of days, the enthusiasm had been deflated. The zeal wasn't quite what he expected from himself. He hadn't even spent time in his Bible for a few days.

Hoover and its fans brought pressure, but that paled in comparison to the pressure he put on himeslf. He expected to reach state championship games and win them. More importantly, he expected his players to play to their potential, as individuals and as a team.

Both losses, and the way in which they happened, made him reexamine himself and the Hoover program.

For most coaches, reaching the state championship game two years in a row would be a career height.

During his college years, when he considered transferring from Southern Miss to Alabama, he relied on scripture from the book of Joshua.

On this December day, he reached for his Bible again and turned to the book of Jeremiah. In the 29th chapter, he found these words:

> **"For I know the plans I have for you, declares the Lord. Plans for good and not for evil, to give you a future and a hope."**

Josh, once again, felt comfort, peace, and inspiration only felt when he was close to God.

Motivated again, Josh set out to become better than he had ever been before...as a man, a father, a husband, and a coach. He dedicated his work to a heightened standard of excellence. He resolved to prepare his players and coaches in a more thorough and efficient way than ever before.

The result?

Since that December morning of 2011, when the word of God inspired Josh to pursue excellence with a passion greater than ever, the great has become even greater.

That morning was clearly a life-changing day for Josh Niblett.

Today can be an equally pivotal moment for you.

There are some things you will have to do today. You may have to go to work or school. You'll have to obey traffic signals if you drive. You'll have to pay sales tax if you buy something. You have to breathe if you're going to live.

But there's one thing you don't have to do today.

You don't have to end this day as the same person you were when you began it.

You can change.

Josh rededicated himself to excellence through service to God and others. He rededicated himself to be an even better steward of the things God had given him.

You can do that too.

Today.

Go ahead and read Jeremiah 29, or at least re-read the verse above. It's a great opportunity for you to realize that God loves you and wants the best for you.

Just as Coach Josh Niblett leads the Hoover Bucs through each season, you can use this book to be coached by him and the standard of excellence that has brought many championships.

Remember...those who are the best still receive coaching. The best golfers, including Tiger Woods during his prime years, received lessons every week. The best hitters in Major League Baseball are coached on their skills on a daily basis. Even the best quarterbacks in the NFL routinely receive coaching.

If it's good enough for them, it can be good enough for you.

Josh Niblett didn't search inside himself because he lost two championship games; he searched because he thought he could do better.

Two Decembers later, after winning their 30th straight game and second consecutive state championship, a reporter asked Josh about the accomplishments of the Hoover team. With a smile, and with fatherly pride for his players, he proclaimed that this team, in the glorious history of Hoover High School, was "better...than ever before."

You, too, can be better...than ever before.

You, too, can have Tunnel Vision.

WHY NOT ME??

FROM THE
SMOKE-FILLED
TUNNEL
**PREPARE FOR
SUCCESS**

EXCELLENCE

HAPPINESS

JOIN JOSH NIBLETT
IN READING BOOKS
THAT WILL RENEW
YOUR MIND

PURSUE

SUCCESS

THE HOOVER
WAY
CAN ALSO BE YOUR
WAY

Why Not Me?

It's a fair question...one that perhaps we all should ask more often.

In an earlier chapter, you read about the importance of becoming a victor rather than a victim.

Victims just ask: Why me?

Victors ask: Why NOT me?

Who do you want to become? What do you not want to become? What would you like to do with your life? How would you like to make a difference in this world?

Why not you?

Why should you not achieve your dreams? Why should you not excel at what you do? Why can you not become all that God intended for you to be? Why can't you have an impact on others? Why can't you work to heal relationships, plow through painful circumstances, and reach new heights?

Why not you?

In a world filled with strife...where people fight and kill...where crime and underachievement root out dreams and goals like bad weeds...is it possible to live in peace with God and within yourself?

Why not you?

If you haven't done your best in school or at work, and you decide today to devote yourself to excellence and become something different...

Why not you?

If you have parents, or your own children, whom you can impact through your behavior, your beliefs, and your example...

Why not you?

If you haven't taken good care of your body, but want to shape up and make the best of the body that God has given to you...

Why not you?

If you have unintentionally become a victim, asking why...and want to grab life by the horns and become a victor...

Why not you?

Consider the story of Mr. Strauss. He had lost everything...or so he thought.

In 1849, gold was discovered in California. Almost overnight, small settlements became large towns. The local people had no chance to plan, and there weren't enough restaurants, hotels, or even clothes to go around.

Enter Mr. Strauss.

Mr. Strauss left his home in Germany, having invested everything he had to start a new life in America. He made tents, and he brought fine tent material to sell to people who had come to California in the gold rush, because miners needed somewhere to sleep.

When he arrived, Strauss had no success; few of the miners wanted to buy his material for tents.

It appeared that he had risked everything...and lost.

After much prayer and contemplative thought, he decided to look at things a different way. Mr. Strauss began asking miners what they needed, and many of them told him that they needed tougher pants for the difficult conditions involved with mining gold. The new mindset transformed Levi Strauss, who created the first blue jeans.

The rest, as they say, is history.

SO WHAT'S IN IT FOR ME?

Yes, the story about Levi Strauss bluejeans is interesting...even entertaining...but how does that affect you?

If you have a Bible, please turn it to the book of Romans. If you don't have a Bible, check out the website BibleGateway.com and search the 12th chapter of Romans.

In the first paragraph of that chapter, God tells us to "transform ourselves by the renewing of our minds."

What does that mean?

Levi Strauss could have given up, but instead, he began looking at things in a different way.

He renewed his mind.

For you, the 12th chapter of Romans gives you the roadmap to changing your life. You see, what you become and who you become is between you and God. Nobody else can make that decision other than you and your Creator.

Through God's power, you can renew your mind.

Through God's power, you can transform yourself.

Through God's power, you can become free from those

relationships that burden you but don't define you.

You are not your past.

You are not your past mistakes.

You are not your past grades.

You are not your past wins, losses, or statistics.

You are God's child...fearfully and wonderfully made.

If you want excellence in your life, nothing stands between you and God.

If you want excellence in your career, nothing stands between you and your Creator.

If you want excellence, but don't see a direction or purpose, that same Bible you're reading now will be God's method of showing you the way.

Just focus, and remain focused, on your destination and your relationship with God.

Just keep your Tunnel Vision.

Tunnel Vision

Chapter 9

Focus on Your Mind

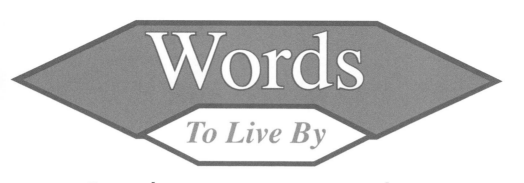

Coach   Josh
Niblett
Some Favorite Bible Verses

One of the keys to Coach Josh Niblett's success, both on and off the field, is his daily time in the Word of God. As you have already read, Josh turned to the Word of God at crucial times in his life. As always, he found guidance and wisdom in scripture. While you strive for excellence through Tunnel Vision, please enjoy, think through, and even memorize some of Coach's favorite Bible verses.

2 Timothy Chapter 4, Verse 2
"Preach the word; be prepared in season and out of season; correct, rebuke and encourage—with great patience and careful instruction."

Proverbs Chapter 27, Verse 17
"As iron sharpens iron, so one person sharpens another."

Jeremiah Chapter 29, Verse 11
"For I know the plans I have for you," declares the Lord, "plans to prosper you and not to harm you, plans to give you hope and a future."

Joshua Chapter 1, Verse 9
"Have I not commanded you? Be strong and courageous. Do not be afraid; do not be discouraged, for the Lord your God will be with you

Coach Josh Niblett
Favorite Bible Verses
(continued)

2 Timothy Chapter 1, Verse 7
"For God has not given us a spirit of fear, but of power and of love and of a sound mind."

Psalm 37, Verse 4
"Delight yourself also in the Lord, and He shall give you the desires of your heart."

Galatians Chapter 6, Verse 9
"And let us not grow weary while doing good, for in due season we shall reap if we do not lose heart."

PLEASE DO THIS

Please read one verse, spending 5 minutes thinking about it and asking God to use His word to change you. There are 7 verses, and if you spend 5 minutes each day with a different verse, you can do it again the next week. You'll be spending time with your Creator, and you'll begin to transform yourself by renewing your mind.

Coach Josh Niblett
Favorite Books

Good To Great
Why Some Companies Make the Leap...and Others Don't
by James C. Collins

Urban's Way
Urban Meyer, the Florida Gators, and His Plan to Win
by Urban Meyer

Win Forever
Live, Work, and Play Like a Champion
by Pete Carroll

How Good Do You Want To Be?
A Champion's Tips on How to Lead and Succeed
in Work and in Life
by Nick Saban, Brian Curtis (With), Bill Belichick (Foreword by)

Tunnel Vision

Chapter 10

in Focus

The Niblett family, at Christmas time, in the home they open to all Hoover Bucs players each week. Karon and Josh Niblett seek to teach their children to give of their time, talents, and resources. Pictured front row L-R are Karon, Sky, and Josh. In the back row, L-R, are Harper and Shaw.

In his first head coaching job, Josh Niblett led Oneonta High School to the state championship. Josh poses with his son, Shaw, who has grown considerably since this photo.

By the time the Niblett family posed on the field at Josh's second head coaching job (at historic Oxford High School), his career and family had expanded.

Excellence
The Next Generation of Tunnel Vision

(Right) Josh and daughter Harper celebrate her team's trophy as state runner-up in the 10-and-under soft-ball championships.

(Above) Shaw Niblett (right) and father Josh celebrate Shaw's championship won on the gridiron by Bumpus Middle School.

(Right) Sky Niblett (right) and father Josh celebrate Sky's championship won on the gridiron in the 95 lb. youth league.

Karon and Josh Niblett celebrate 2013 Bucs Day at the
Riverchase Galleria. As always, Bucs fans support every
event involving the team.

The Nibletts enjoy the University of Alabama's 2013 homecoming, which marked
the 20th anniversary of Josh's first season of playing time for the Crimson Tide.

Under the stadium lights, Karon and Josh Niblett
celebrate another win by his Hoover Bucs. Josh
will say, early and often, that Karon is his teammate
in all areas of life.

John Niblett (right) joins his son Josh on the field for a
Hoover Bucs practice.

Josh (left) dons a ball cap and chews on a cigar as he plays coach to his older brother Tad.

Niblett brothers Josh (left) and Tad (right) prepare to lead their dad's team to victory.

Brenda Niblett (standing) poses with her family, including husband John (seated, center), Josh (left), Heather (seated), and Tad (standing, right).

Josh Niblett began his collegiate career at the University of Southern Mississippi before transferring to the University of Alabama.

The original Niblett children (L-R), Heather, Josh, and Tad

Tad (left) and Josh (right).

Tad Niblett,
with his wife
Paige, daughter
Cassidy, and son
Riley.

Heather is joined by
her husband Bob and
their children Reese,
Carter, and Graham.

95

Josh and Karon after the 2013 state championship victory.

Only one grade apart in school, Josh and Heather both excelled on the basketball court, as well as in other sports and in the classroom.

Tunnel Vision

Chapter 11

The Fruits of Focus

Coach Josh Niblett

The Fruits of His Labor

The Oneonta Redskins

Season	Wins	Losses	Result
2000	5	6	1st round playoffs
2001	7	4	1st round playoffs
2002	11	2	3rd round playoffs
2003	13	2	State runner-up Lost to Pike County
2004	15	0	STATE CHAMPIONS

The Oxford Yellow Jackets

Season	Wins	Losses	Result
2005	5	6	1st round playoffs
2006	6	5	1st round playoffs
2007	10	0	

**In 2007, an ineligible player caused the forfeiture of seven games.

Coach Josh Niblett

The Fruits of His Labor

The Hoover Bucs

Season	Wins	Losses	Result
2008	13	2	State runner up lost to Prattville
2009	14	1	STATE CHAMPIONS
2010	14	1	State runner up lost to Daphne
2011	13	2	State runner up lost to Prattville
2012	15	0	STATE CHAMPIONS
2013	15	0	STATE CHAMPIONS **NATIONAL CHAMPIONS

The Niblett family thanks you for your time in learning about commitment to honoring our Lord and Savior Jesus Christ. We look forward to hearing from you as you study the path to excellence through *Tunnel Vision*.

Thank You...from G. Tom Ward

Listed alphabetically by first names:

Betty and Gary Ward...whose contributions to this book, and hours of support, are innumerable...thank you for your Tunnel Vision in helping in so many ways.

Dr. Buddy Gray...for giving time, encouragement, and spiritual guidance to a project with the same enthusiasm and humility with which you lead.

David Bannister...for insisting that a writer meet a coach because they reminded him of each other.

Dorothy Ward...for playing a critical role in making this project possible, and for powerful prayer at opportune times.

Glenn Waddell...whose encouragement, in critical times, resonates far beyond what he might have imagined.

Heather Niblett Rickman...for sharing your classic stories, memories, time, and knowledge in a way that added greatly to this book.

James Ward....for devoting your knowledge of sports & sports marketing to empowering this project to succeed.

Dr. Jane Geiger...for being there for every moment of this book's birth, for originating the *Tunnel Vision* idea, for being the only Miss Vestavia to edit two Hoover books, and for making all things in my life better...than ever before.

John & Brenda Niblett...for time, expertise, photographs, support, and prayer. For the two of you, giving of yourselves is routine.

Josh, Karon, Shaw, Harper, & Sky Niblett...family, friends, teammates, and fellow ministers. Thanks for using this book to share your family and *Tunnel Vision* with others.

Tad Niblett...for sharing your time, unique perspective, and football knowledge. Thanks also for sharing your childhood and family with all readers of this book.

Notes

Notes